I Want a Poem

I Want a Poem

and Other Poems

JERRY PINTO

SPEAKING TIGER

SPEAKING TIGER BOOKS LLP
125 A, Ground Floor, Shahpur Jat, Near Asiad Village
New Delhi 110049

Published by Speaking Tiger Books 2021

ISBN: 978-93-90477-61-6
eISBN: 978-93-90477-74-6

10 9 8 7 6 5 4 3 2 1

Typeset in EB Garamond by SÜRYA, New Delhi
Printed at

Dedication:
This one is for Nissim, Adil, Arun and Eunice.
(Hang in there, Adil!)

Apologia:
'We publish so as not to spend our lives correcting drafts.'

—Borges, quoting Reyes to Osvaldo Ferrari
(*Conversations 1*, Seagull Books)

CONTENTS

Memory Box

Memory box, memory box,
Battened down with several locks,
Memory box, memory box,
Full of dreary little shocks.

What to remember
What to forget
What to care to remember
What to try to forget
What to put down
What to hide in full sight?

Memory box, one day I'll take you down to the river
And I'll open you up and in full view of the fish, they'll
Come tumbling out, cobwebby, guilty and gilded.
I'll call some poetry, I'll call some prose.
The others I'll set down on a leaf, a dry leaf
And camphor-blaze them into the sunset.

House Repairs

All it took was the flick of a chisel
And the bathroom wall came sighing down.
It wasn't quite what we had hoped for
But we took it for what it was:
One more act
in a prolonged dramaturgy
of cement.

The new wall came up quickly.
Overnight, it was back in place.
It was all that a new wall should be
Or so we hoped.

Only, the next morning and the next
When, sleep-clogged, we lurched into it
We found it was our old wall.
With a suicide note still scrawled on it
The blood still fresh on it.

We paid the masons anyway
And learned something about renovation.

Drawing Home

Were I to draw my home, I don't think
I would do it quite like this drawing of yours.
All these right angles and hinges bear no resemblance
To my memories of suddenness and curves, odd shapes
And our balancing act: four on a trapeze.
Still, I don't resent your drawing.
I rather like it, in fact; this way of making coherent
Scenes of such randomness.

You could play one camera. I could be the other.
We could ask for a neutral third so that
Between the three of us, we'd miss nothing.
You could go for the big picture; I have an eye for nuance.
The third camera, full-frontal, unblinking
Could mediate. We might arrive at something
Between your version and mine.

Litany

Like all efficient litanies
It has rhythms.
It lets you pray laterally
As your lips work the words.

Like all good litanies
It works better on your knees;
Easy to say and
Uneasy to believe.

Like all powerful litanies
It allows for choral recitation.
It can be soporific
Letting you forget what it really means.

Like all old litanies
It comes with a history.
Augustine of Hippo, church father,
unwilling bishop, pear-stealer
author, alchemist
begetter of bastard sons
and my dastard litany:
Not yet, not yet.

Backstairs, Elphinstone College

I thought you belonged with me here
On the metal stairs that crouched
Like a diseased relative, in the corners of the big
Brownstone building, meant for posterity, built for ceremony.
I thought you saw the point:
No sweep, no banister, no grand ascension,
But functional, rising, getting there all the same.

But one day I saw how you owned the stone ceremonial
Of the main stairs; how your knee rose in helium-filled
Right angles of leg and stair turned swastika of unearned
And unlearned privilege; I turned and tossed my burning body
Down the metal stairs (the metal staircase allows for Romantic
Gestures the main staircase would laugh at), past the rotting paper
Smell of archive and library, past the deep red smell of the toilet,
Past the pigeon droppings and old excrescences of collegiate desire,
Past balled-up love letters, past you and me facing upwards,
First love intoxicated in a chemistry class in which the only
        good thing
Was the organic equation of thigh against thigh.

Past the first precipitous flights, I slowed down
And I could hear myself clattering, settling, crouching
Like a diseased relative, one step, one step down,
          down past the past,
Down, down, one step at a time, one hobbling step at a time,
Getting there all the same.

Tomorrow

All those Os.
All those warm round egg Os.
All those finities, all those certainties.
All those closures, enclosures, complete.
Even the O made of thumb tacks and duct tape.

Nothing but Os.
Surprise and jouissance.
Nothing but outwardness all round.

And a mirror image
On its head.

Tomorrow.

Ctrl-Alt-Dlt

So easy to delete, backspace, or even
in extremis
Ctrl-Alt-Dlt all at once.

Ctrl
The illusion
slips away
if you look at it
directly.

Alt
Against the parallel universes,
the parallel possibilities
the parallel lives.

Dlt
Does not exist.

'Will You Miss Me?'

Let me see.
How shall I miss you? Let me count the ways.

I shall miss you as a broken needle misses its thread.
I shall miss you as the bones of Nureyev miss his jetés.
I shall miss you as Beckham missed his penalty in 2004.
I shall miss you as ISRO misses Chandrayaan.

And I shall miss you as I would a stone in my shoe.
And I shall miss you as New York misses its twins.
I shall miss you as I would miss a splint in my shins.
Oh yes, in those ways too.

But I shall miss me too
Shall miss how you made me.
I shall miss what we made of each other.
The stain of your voice in mine.
The phrase I fed you one evening.
The outpost I still man in your mind.
The anicut you built in mine.

I wish I could say I would not miss you so much because of this.
This coming and going, this uncanny symbiosis, this more than
friendship,

This more bizarre than love, this sense of a connection forged
before we met.
I wish I could say: you're in me, I'm in you, what's to miss, who
to miss?

But I'm not that way.
I will miss you.
Some days it will be bad.
Some days will open into darkness and only music
or chocolate
or yoga
or language
will lighten them.
Some days will close into darkness in which I will store up
things to tell you
and lose sleep,
panicking that I
might forget.
And there will be other days when it will only be a moment
When something opens up and oozes.

Hold on.

I will miss you.
But you're going away.
I'm here.
If you don't want to be missed, stay.

No.
You're off.
You're a truck without brakes running down a hill road.
You're a comet being whipped around by some dark sun.
You're what you want to be.
You're off.
I'm staying.
And you're asking, 'Will you miss me?'

You have some cheek.
I will miss that cheek.
I will miss you.
I don't have much choice.

Window

What can you do with a window?
It will always remain four-cornered
Always be a savagery to the sky
Always offer enough room for only one head
Or one cloud.

There's nothing open about a window.

Our Trade

I suppose I could lie
It's easily done and can be forgiven
As long as the lie is good and smooth
And leavened with a touch of the truth.
What's fiction but a lie well told?
I could lie but the truth is
Our trade begins in magic.

What's the use of saying silence helps?
Noise may help too. The call of the cuckoo
I hear thee and rejoice
Or the stuttering orisons of...but you know that one.
No use framing a law that contradicts itself.
Even in our trade.

But I offer you a contradiction instead:
All words disrupt silence
But the only ones that echo
Are born in the silence they destroy.

It could be the flaming of a flower at noon
The ancient red unease at the full moon

The startling indeterminacy of dusk
Or a lost lover's intimate musk.
If you can't remember, go ahead,
Invent.

There are some letters about this somewhere
If I can find them...no.
You'll have to do without.
I warn you, there's a lot of doing without
In this trade.

It wasn't always like that.
There was a time we were stars.
Rock stars? Nothing to us then
They only want to fuck rock stars.
Us they wanted to swallow whole,
Such was the yearning.

For it was not a story we told
But flesh we put on their bones.
We turned them round and showed them
Who they were and who they could be.

We were memory. We were history.
We were ritual. We were community.
We held the secrets. We told their lies.
We were monstrance. We were scroll.

We were labyrinth. We were sanctum.
We were spire. We were libation.
We were all they needed,
And when the moon was full and silver
As the coins they dropped into our bowls
We invented their world.
What am I saying?
We invented *them*.

We're still at it.
Only the reinvention business is a little crowded these days.
Our hieroglyphs aren't profane enough
Our ancientness not new enough
Our black-and-white is blurry grey.
Don't go there. Don't even try.
What is real is this. You. Me.
And between us not even enough money for a cutting chai
And a cigarette.

Don't smoke?
You'll find your vice.
Only, don't let it be words.

Words, words, words, he said 400 years ago
Even before the pocket book revolution.
What do you think he'd say now as the words
Pour in a sludgy militant flood out of every profligate mouth?

Which is why we sit alone on this lonely arid plateau called language
And we drop our turdwords to fertilise
The soil for the bankers and milliners and armies
For the sandpaper tongues that buff our jagged edges.

And at the end, there are no guarantees
The jungles outlive us.
Our lines die with us.
The worst shall be first.
And the bile with which we sought to cure the world
Turns toxic in our throats.

So I have a word of advice for you:
RUN.

Seven Types of Anger

The first: rehearsal rage.
Pacing the streets, an internal tirade
Aimed at love and only love:
lovers, family, friends.
All turned dumb and guilty,
Stricken by the knowledge that
Behind my impenetrable façade
Of logic-as-I-construe-it
I am in tears.

The second: the quick acid spurt at the self
Always such a tempting object,
Such a sitting duck.
The alkaline self redux
Turns all into the salt and water
Of self-pity.

The third: shimmering
quivering
shaking
sweating
incoherence.

It breaks down here: who's counting?
Saboteur, saviour, sucker,
Naming you does not help.
You're not dead yet.

A Poem, Freighted with Anger

A poem, freighted with anger,
rarely flies. Instead,
it lumbers off the page
and fails before it
reaches. It grinds to a halt.
But as it rusts,
on the *khud*,
small animals take shelter.
Valley children,
lean-limbed, leather-footed,
climb in, take the wheel,
learn to dream.

Colours

1

Under the shade of a great tree,
In the middle of an old forest,
It must be different.
The small scrabblings, the sieved light,
Earthscent of old moult and aborted germinations.
Roots deep, deep, as far beneath as
New-born sunlit leaves overhead.
Think of the great heaving of water up and up...
If on some grey rainy day, I should need
To trust the uninflected yellow of butterflies
Look for me in the middle of an old forest.

2

My dark dolphin undertow,
Old friend, sinuous, amoeboid
Unstinting companion, faithful shadow
Don't look now.
I have exchanged my eyes for prisms.
The exorcism is about to begin.

3

My patrimony includes a green glass duck
With blushing toe-nails and sanguine beak,
Forever open, as though to speak.

It gives me to understand however
That it will crack first.

Day duck: a silent oracle
Night duck's toenails click on the shelf
It is now afloat on a swamp
Where it must feed before morning
As the minnows sink down to the sludge.

The swamp is part of my patrimony
By family tradition, I keep it wet.
I feed it from my veins:
Our family swamp of which we are proud.

4

In my father's eyes
I saw how a man
Who said he was tone-deaf
Could hear the blues.

Today My Mother Is in the Audience

Today my mother is in the audience
As she never was when she lived.
Today, she sits in the audience and I see
Her as whole, as at her best, a mischievous
Twinkle in her eye, a twinkle that says,
'Chhuh baba, don't let these people see
Your pompous side.'

She loved the English language, my mother,
Who knew Burmese until her Goan cousins
Laughed her into amnesia and gave her
the gift of Konkani and some Portuguese.
In this audience, my mother smiles when
A smile is called for. She loves it when
You clap or laugh. It embarrasses me,
That smile, her clear uninflected enjoyment
Of any small success. I bear it bravely
Because she is somewhere in the audience.

Family Tree

Any clear-eyed botanist
Would condemn you.
Your best yields are past;
Many strange fruit dangle
From the lower boughs, ankles
Turning in tightening circles.
Your shade is niggardly too.

But we still belong as a matter of course
And the tree lives on, of course.
As its wizened seeds stray off course.

The Psychopathology of a Child's Drawing

You did not draw a house, boy.
You drew yourself.
Your head keeps the cloud out and blots out the sun.
Your roof is pointy, a triangle.
Your thoughts will remain in the attic, boy, and gather dust.
You are safe, tiled, tarred and
The last few feathers are drying under the eaves.
Your eyes are windows.
They are closed. Why close your eyes?
You precious shit, did you add curtains?
That mouth is closed too.
Your tongue comes slipping, sliding, slithering
Out into the world of utterance.
Your house is two-dimensional
It has no room
It has no backstory.
Yet smoke rises from your chimney.
What burns?

The Parable of Xeroxo and Xeroxa

Of course, Xeroxa knew she was mythical;
So did Xeroxo but in a less tangible way.
Any thinking person, entity, clone or photocopy
Knows this for a fact; inasmuch as a fact can be
Allowed for in the saying of 'in fact' (or fax).

This did not stop Xeroxo from wanting to replicate.
It gave Xeroxa pause but only once a cartridge.
'The only fear,' she said to the brand manager,
'Is decay of information.'
'Fight your genes,' said God.

Missing

Those yellow butterflies like debutantes, more perk than purpose.
Mugs, white mugs with navy blue trim, for men to drink
        morning tea from.
Scapulars showing against the reednecks of duckback girls in
        faded indigo uniforms.
The mothball scent of old suits and old spice at weddings.
Dictionaries, atlases, books that manufactured meaning.
The blouseless lady who scraped the grinding stone raw,
        tunktunktunk
And the spice girls who pounded chillies to powder, thuck,
        thook, thuck, thook.
A sense of belonging, uninflected by questions,
        undisturbed by purpose,
Last seen in cloth diapers (full), heading back to milk-smeared
        mother-breast.

In Ours

(In answer to the eternal Indian question: How is it in yours?)

In ours
We marry only those
With kneecaps undented
Lips indented
Histories invented.

In ours
God chooses who we should
Marry and then we
Tell a priest who can extract
A reasonable sum.

In ours
A child is not born
We say, one less on that side
And a new insurance policy
Is made out in
The father's name.

In ours
We don't fuss if a child
Won't eat fruit.
We don't take it as a sign.
We're not like that.

In ours
When someone dies
Her eldest son will carry
Pebbles in his pockets and
Act normal, very normal.

In ours
We don't mention D.
We say, 'He left his fizzy
drink and went out for
Coconut water.'

In ours,
when a man dies
his eldest son applies
For paternity leave.

In ours
We do.
We so do.

In ours
flowers are seen
as acts of violence.
BAM.

In ours
We often do.
We do so.

If She Did the Safe Thing

If she did the safe thing,
If she went home and had a cup of tea instead;
Or bought herself a silk scarf;
Or another kind of lily, refusing advice;
Or if she told the old lady, no, she was not all right;
Or if she phoned home and asked for a lift,
She would not be someone in fiction.

She would be someone who drank tea instead,
The pink satin negligee unused,
The flashlight untested.

Functions of an Audience, Discerned After a Long Apprenticeship as a Member Thereof, at Various Cultural Events

To clap with energy
To laugh without irony
To make eye contact
To be there at the beginning
To be alive at the end
To leave
To take with you your debris
To go
To disappear
Now.

And When

And when they opened his head, to air the room, through the eyes winds blew in and out came cotton-ball clouds of old thought but before anyone could net them or pin them down or flashfreeze them or even photograph them, they dissolved and left us all clutching at each other, lost anthologists of the thoughts of others.

This has now happened so often that we have decided that only one last poem can be written about it and then we'll stop, all of us, you too in the back, scribbling away to get yours done before this one.

If that works, it works. If it doesn't work, we have only the Other Way. And we're not going there, not without insurance and a glass-bottomed boat.

The Teeth of a Movie Star

I want to spend just one decade
With the teeth of a movie star.
This is a metaphor.

I want now to care about surface
And since surface has no place for
The depthiness and interioration of metaphor
I want to spend one decade
With a movie star smile.

I want to spend one decade of my life
(My own life, with my consciousness)
As a movie star who doesn't have to make movies.
I want to flash and shine and slide and chick-tick.
I want to raise champagne flutes all cold, pale gold
Warm brandy balloons in my palms and moon the paparazzi.
I want to consume recklessly. I want more than my fair
Share of the world's time and money and energy and space
And beauty. I want.

Now in the dentist's waiting room with a bleeding stump
I am so far from this dream that I can dream it with
No guilt, no pain, no me.

I Want a Poem

I want a poem like thick tropical rain.
Dense green spatter of syllables,
Drumbeat consonants, fertile with meaning.
Sudden. Short. Unforgettable.
Afterwards, jungle silence.

I want a poem like a Russian circus;
You should know it has been trained.
No ordinary everyday poem could leap like that,
No quotidian poem could shimmer, spangle, exult like that.
Oh satin, yes, and yes, fakery, and then
Popcorn applause and a lonely child,
Big-eyed, dreaming of running away to the poem.

I want a poem like an animal.
You should be able to eat it. Or domesticate it.
You should be able to befriend it. Or behead it.
You could carry it around or make it bear your burdens.
You could, should, oh should, so should, clean up after it.
Afterwards: Skeleton poem rides in night terror through
ice-cream cloud cover.

I want a poem.
I want a poem.
I get instead this poem.
A poem of clanking wants like a pile of bhaandi-bartan going
over a waterfall in a barrel,
A poem of whispering needs like a tree whose branches scrape
plea-bargains from the pavement as it is dragged
to the bonfire.

I want a poem
like a chorus of angels,
a chamber of horrors,
a block buster film,
a sexcapade with candlewax,
an anaconda adventure,
a ride in a Batmobile,
a contessa in a fountain.
I want a poem.

Buying Words

I would too
I would buy words.
I would buy them compulsively.
I would buy them impulsively.
I would buy them from other tongues.
I would buy them wet with saliva.
I would buy leaf-skeleton words, flesh boiled off the bone,
I would mate them with bulgy sexy words,
        slippery-straddle-thrust words
I would.

I would buy words for later, when like A L Kennedy
I might need them in a hotel room after a bullfight.

I would buy some now to use immediately,
ripping the packet open with my teeth, even before I got home.

I would buy some from myself were I to meet some younger J
        upon a golden beach.
(He had quite a store.)

I would buy words because you can't eat words
but I sell words that I may eat.

I would buy words in air-conditioned malls and from wayside stalls.

I would buy words for you too.
I would buy words for all of us to use.
No word would be mine alone.
That would be to squander it.
We could have joint custody.
I might keep some words all week
But I would be good about weekends.
And you could have some for
The whole summer vacation.

But you should know this.
I would make a list.
And I would count.
I would count mostly to know if I had got
My money's worth out of the words I bought.

But on mean-spirit days, I would count to see if you
Had got more use out of words of my money than I had.

Then the next morning, I'd buy some more again.

My Poems

My poems are about many things.
My poems are about magic.
My poems are about music.
My poems are about poetry festivals.
My poems are written for people like you.
My poems take short cuts; my poems ride slipstreams
My poems take the path of least resistance.
My poems are needy.
My poems need you to like them.
My poems want you to remember them.
My poems demand that you should memorise them.
My poems want prizes.
My poems want to be on syllabi and curricula.
My poems want to be translated into Hindi, Marathi, Tamil,
        Telugu, Gujarati, Sanskrit, German, French, Italian,
        Polish, Afrikaans
        and American.
My poems want diplomatic immunity.
My poems want visa on arrival.
My poems want to be burned in public but only by men
        in the right kind of clothes.
My poems want exclusion from the canon and recovery by
        Pound, Eliot or Rushdie.
My poems want to be epigraphs to other poems.

My poems want to be photographs of busty blondes
        with smooth silky thosethings.
My poems challenge virtual reality.
My poems are live headlines and red bottomlines.
My poems want you to sit up and pay attention in pin-drop
        silence or they'll come and get you.
My poems are torn from the gut and mined in the amygdale.
My poems are dredged from the heart and filed in the
        sigmoid colon.
My poems are seeds planted in your head; they'll sprout
        when you're dead.
My poems are viruses; they self-replicate, they do that
        parthenogenesis thing.
My poems are programmes, they'll erase your hard disk
        and implode.
My poems are dangerous. They can only be bought by
        adults who have certificates of
                illiteracy that make them immune.
My poems are wanted by Interpol.
My poems are tracked by the FBI.
My poems are protected by Amnesty International.

Thank God I am nothing like my poems.

Inside

Inside, I'm a slattern.
Inside, there are dust motes in every eye.
And every eye a wound.
And every wound a metaphor
And in each metaphor, a wealth of meaning.
Inside me Miss Havisham meets Saleem Sinai
They fall in love and run seven times around
The island and mistake it for marriage.

Inside, I'm a convict
And I've locked up some devices and desires:
    In a box that has a gold key, a silver key, a lead key,
    You get to choose and you get your speech time
    But oh dear, oh dear, oh dear,
    It's always the wrong key and your balls go
    So you will sing a higher octave
    Even if it's the same key.

    And there's rage in a vial that seems quite dry
    Like the bull pee that dasturs pray over,
    Like vials of blood that liquefy for feasts and priests.

    And desire like a ring to be slipped
    Through the nose of the double bull
    So it can be taken to market.

Inside, I'm a bird
My bones are light
And my nest contains broken stories
That I must feed every hour.
But I can soar and plummet
And shit where I want.

Inside me, I'm an estate
I have not been admitted to probate.
I am actually of such immense value
That I have no value at all.

Inside me, I'm a lake: still, cold, dreamstruck.
Inside me, I like it here.

Wish I could stay.
Wish you were here.

Weeding

My back a bow in an Ardenhout garden
To clear weeds from a rosebush bed.
I am playing good guest;
But my sympathies are with the weeds.

'No, no, Jerry, don't break the stems.
They'll just grow back. Rock them
Back and forth. Be gentle [but ruthless];
Loosen the roots. Right. Like that.
Now rinse off the good soil.
Bring them to the compost heap.'

Here their amino acids may start a new life.
And if they have been good weeds
May they reap the karma of their good deeds—
Be reborn to blush and fade as rosebushes do.

My sympathy is with the weeds.
Small, green, tenacious, unaware of the
Hierarchies of horticulture, they sprout.
Unwanted, but how are they supposed to know?

So I rock and I rinse
I rock and I rinse.

And under my breath, I say:
'If I should ever have a garden...'

I do not complete the promise
It is time for dinner and a soufflé will not keep.

Grief

For Mehlli Gobhai (1931-2018)

A useful device, the cinematic dissolve:
Deployed with basic skill, it can swiftly resolve
Everyman's problem: the tedium of grieving.
Slice here, splice there, and now you're leaving
Long hours of apathy on the editing floor.
Those days when your sorrow is only a bore—
Not just to those too well-bred to tell
How you're making their lives a living Hell
But even, admit it, to yourself as well.

Here, grief is a shell, lying on a beach,
Stranded by the tide, as if out of the reach
Of grace and faith's consoling illogic.
Here time isn't slow, its pace is geologic.

This script was not written to please you.
This edit wasn't designed to ease you.

We Need More Words for Rain

What is the word for remembered rain?
For rain remembered as the stain of blood?

What is the word for the sound of rain?
The tickettytack on the window pane?
The thoock-thapack on the coffin lid?
What is the word for the sound of rain?

What is the name of the rain you want to forget?
Rain cold, rain bleak, rain without, rain within.

What is the rain that still hides between your thighs?
What is the name of cliché-clot rain?

Yes, you did.
Yes, you welcomed the rain.
Yes, you walked hand-in-hand
Yes, you laughed and drank raindrops
(and said something silly like,
'This tastes like water'
and your lover drank it from
your mouth and said, 'It tastes
like you' and you laughed and said
'I taste like rain.')

Yes, you did.

What is the word for the feeling you had
When you were waist-deep in the sea
And it began to rain, a hymn to grey?
                    Old men called from the beach
                    Old women told their beads
And you? You said, 'Yes, pray for me.
This grey is me. And so is the sea
And the raindrop is me
And this might explain
Why I no longer see
Where the horizon is: that line
Between sky and sea
Between eye and me

Yes, pray for me.
Yes, maybe even,
Pray to me.'

What does moss call rain?
What does beach call rain?
What does Homeless call rain?
What does desert call rain?
What does paper call rain?
What does rain call rain?

We need more words for rain.

On Seeing a Friend's Post Featuring a Young Man in a Bespoke Suit on His Way to His Standard Ten Farewell Party

I don't know why I should want to cry for you, young man in a beautiful bespoke suit.
You and I have nothing in common. You wear your suit to the manner born. I still don't have one. You want to go to this party; I didn't want to go to mine. I didn't trust groups of men; still don't.
But I know something of what is going on inside your head. I know you have new underwear on as an act of faith. I know how you will want to laugh at your own hopes when you peel them off tomorrow morning, unseen by anyone other than yourself; how you will also want to cry.
I know that you shaved and wondered why you were shaving when your cheeks are still smooth. It's something about cream and foam and blade—this concatenation that feels so male. It will be some time before you see it as a botheration. You didn't nick yourself as far as I can see. At your age, I left my face blood-flecked each time I shaved but we didn't have five blades pressed close, intimately; pentupled killing.
Killing? Killing.
That's what we're known for, that's how we're seen.
Armed and dangerous.

That penis you have tucked away and which you wished, ritually, was two inches longer? That's our weapon. Every day, the newspaper brings fresh tidings of how we've turned another woman's body into a bloody playground for our resentful longings.
Your suit is camouflage. If I am to judge you by what our kind does, it is for the others I must weep. You, your particular innocence, your specific uneasy expectancy, half-boy-half-man—I should have no time to waste over you.
So let me reach beyond you to those who went before you.

Abhimanyu, I send you out into the world with conflicting messages. I say you must win but I do not tell you how to treat the loser. I say you must be a winner but I do not say that chances are you will lose many more battles than you lose.

David, how many of you will we send out before we can find an end to war? They say you ran to the confrontation. Naked against a giant? You have lived our nightmares for us.

Ephebos, no man is sure, we only play at confidence and we get so good at the game, we forget. When you're finally lowering your trousers in the presence of another, you're not going to be sure how good a lover you're going to be.

Puru, we demand your youth from you. We have nothing to offer in exchange, nothing so precious. Ours is a bad bargain. The only consolation you can have is that many have made it before and many will make it again.

Eklavya, need I remind you that you do not upset the hierarchy? This silencing of a dog with arrows so as to leave your master's tapas unharmed and the dog's mouth unscathed, what were you trying to prove? But he was kind to you when he asked you for your thumb. Meet Talos, whose uncle Daedalos killed him for being too talented. Where did you go, Eklavya, with your bleeding hand?

Nachiketas, have you not learned that the world does not like unsettling questions?
Isaac, look beyond the campfire. Is that a shadow or is that Ishmael, banished for his birth?

Young man in the bespoke suit, I would arm you with my experience, but would it dull those eyes? Would it set your jaw or crush the expectant hunch of your shoulders?
Young man in the bespoke suit, the world will not always be kind to you. But if you can be kind still, if you can bring tenderness and vulnerability to love, one small battle will be won even as the war we wage on those we love rages on.
Meanwhile, go on then, the party is waiting.

Loving, Leaving

I can't even remember when I fell in love with you.
Or how. The best love stories itemise, anatomise.
I know; I've loved them in my time. The sweet impossible
The fragrant improbable; what they said and felt and thought.
What they could not say but thought.
I realised I loved you and that the love had always been there.
It had been waiting for you to become you
And maybe me to become me too and for us
To walk into each other's hearts. I know I walked
Into yours but my place was small. I was not the only
Tenant but I settled into my tenement and ignored
Those who had much more real estate. I let your
Bloodrush enrich my wan and pallid world.
It was so good, I could forget
I loved you and you loved me too.

How did I fall out of love with you?
This I know with preternatural clarity. I can taste
What we were eating; it will always be
Pervaded by the taste of bile. You said something and
I was hurt. I was so hurt, I began to pack my bags.
I was vacating my tenement.
I think you still love me.
I couldn't love you.
Not after what you said.

This is ridiculous, I said to myself, as I unhooked
My various selves from their dusty niches.
Here, my vulnerabilia, through which I spilled secrets,
There, my terribilita, brought on to scare your demons
 into stillness.
I fold up my interest in you
In all the minutiae of your life.
I seal your dossier, the one I had been building
Since I discovered my love for you.
I needed material for it; I needed to populate that
Long slow falling. I needed to know everything:
What you eat and what you don't and what you won't.
How you were in school and how you looked

At each stage of your life. I don't know if I will
Ever need it again but I have it and I don't know what
Use it is now. It will join all the other material
I have collected and which I might never use.
Don't worry about it; it's safe with me.
I don't know how to use it because it reeks
As much of you as of me.

I leave the building. You don't notice.
I did not expect you to but that hurts too.
I look back and there is a flashy sign,
All the colours I could think of:
LOVE, it says in psychedelic fat letters,
1970s letters. I switch the current off.

It is time to turn down the gratitude
I have been shining into the universe for you
And me and us.

I don't understand how this is happening
I don't why I'm vacating, voluntarily vacating
A hearthome I was given and which I made mine.
In all my other vacatings, I have felt:
'Oh you'll be sorry, you'll miss me.'
Not this time. You won't notice my going
I will. I want, even now, to stay but your remark
Sliced the ground out of my tenement.
I found myself in freefall, slowfall, allfall
And my first thought, self-protective thought, was:
When there's nothing left, there's dignity.
And so I am taking my jamjars filled with dreams and...

A single remark.
A single remark?
I'm wondering myself.
Could it be this was so fragile, this intertwining,
this mutuality so mutable that one quip
Was all it took? It was a quip, no?
I know that from the sound of your voice.
I have quipped too.
I should be equipped to deal with that.
I am not.
I find I am not.

Could it be that I did not expect to be hurt?
Could I have been so naïve?
I spent most of my life, braced for pain.
How did I let my guard down?
How did you get past it?
I want to know this for future reference.
And I know that knowing will not help.
The future hurt learns nothing.
The future heart learns nothing.
This is ridiculous, I keep thinking.
Why did you say what you said?
The quip is a call for a response
I'm the one who does things for a response.
So could it be that I invented you
As not-me and so contented myself
With a tenement in your otherness?
Is that why I'm leaving? Can it be so simple?

I am not simple; nor are you.
Together perhaps we were. It happens.
Maybe our complexities cancelled each other out.
Maybe it was all a dream and ended as dreams end.
I wish I knew.
I want so very much to know.
Because I'd understand how I came to love you.
So when I miss that familiar red percussion
Of your blood in my hearthome,
I can retell myself the story of our parting.

One part of me is happy to go.
One part always is.
That part feels free.
That part always does.
Love makes so many demands.
Love insists we be better than that.
Love wants so much more out of us.
Out-of-Love is clear-eyed again.
The self comes knocking.
Hi, old fellow, selfish bastidd,
Cheerful mocker of that which is bigger than you.
Hi, you swine, make yourself comfy.
There'll be further wanderings, yes, yes.
But right now, this part of me belongs to me again.
And that feels good.

Yeah, right.
So why am I crying?
Perhaps this is all it is.
I loved myself enough to leave
The soothing of being loved
For the wrong reasons.

What Remains

What remains is the cool light on end-stopped waves;
And contrapuntal: a mischievous delight in your eye;
A velvet undercoat to your voice,
A shade of green, studied, calculated.

For this meant something, something like stone:
Self-contained, essential, hard-won.
Be serious, it bids me, this stone,
In a way you would never have.

No regrets, says the stone.
No.

Night Lines

Just for this moment, I am of the opinion,
That poetry should be made in bed.
Haan, exactly like that. Just what you're thinking.
Like sex. The same dissolution. The same delight.
The same expectations. The same detritus of
Disappointment and satisfaction and justification.
Hold on a moment while I dust the bed.
Did you hear all those abstract nouns
Fall tinkling—action, iction, ication—to the ground?

Start again. I want to make poetry in bed,
In shorts and jabba.
With chocolate wrappers to attract
Black ant ideas,
Slight, frantic ideas;
Easily lost or squashed ideas,
Not one valuable in itself
But together, a force of nature, yes,
A hive mind more than the individual.

Something primitive about sheets now soft, now slick,
Rich with me.
This me-ness would make the poem thick
Sludgy, capable of what I am capable of.

In bed, my limbs loose and my defences
Rucked up somewhere behind my knees, I am
Capable of so much and so much. Here
I dream and drowse. I plan to die here one day.
No, I don't want this to be a big poem
So I'll stop here and watch this poem
Curl up between my pillow and the wall.

My Biggles Moment

Open to the page: Vitae Lampada
Leave a sign of unfinished business.
The mission is dire, the propeller's afire
And Ginger, you're barmy. Breathes there
The man with balls so dead, who hath not
Chugged raw eggs, his eye that of the tiger,
His silk parachute billowing over the poor blighters
In the trenches? I'd like to be like that
I'd like to laugh at sunburned death
My Adam's apple bobbing as I chug the true, the blushful,
A buddy on my wing and an enemy (The Red Baron?)
Somewhere under the radar's percussive sweep.

Seven Ads for a Dreamerama

1

More.

More and more.

More, much more.

All of it.

More than you need? (Oops)

More than you want? (Never)

Admit it.

You want more.

2

The silk scarf carapace

has a coupon attached.

Post it back to the abyss.

3

We want to wake up.

Blue. Tan. Indigo. Violet.

We want to wake up.

The door to the dreamerama is stuck.

We want to wake up.

Shapeshifters merge with shadowlifters.

There is no waking up.

4

Whatever you do
Avoid the lake of fire.

5

Calm down, the singing ponies said.
They'll cut you some slack, they said.
The last date has been extended.
There's a window open at the back.
Yes, you can earn air miles in the Sylph Realm
But the offer is open only to Gold Card Believers.
Can we see your cheat sheet, please?
Nightmares available at 7 pm, 9 pm or on demand
at a 20 per cent surcharge.

6

There's a ring around the horror.
The oil slick is halfway up the diva's leg.
Your underwear's dreamweave lasts longer, holds stronger.
Intense.
That's what it is.

7

All copy.
Do you copy?
All is copy.
Copy all this.

Walking Away with an Attempt at Grace

(For S, who made the poem happen.

On second thoughts, not for S.

Or for the absence of S? No.

For me

For me and S.

For me and S?

For me without S.)

First came the polite brush-off:
'I'll call you back.'
Then:
'Let's do this Saturday morning?'
And hard on its heels:
'I'm saving a company that's going under.
Talk to you when I'm done.'

I'm paranoid about this kind of thing.
So I wind back to our last meeting.
The front seat of your car.
Bandra and I have work to do.
You are now the kind of person
Who has transcended work.
(Except the occasional saving of a company
Going under during lockdown, no doubt.)

That last meeting is warm.
The parting: warm too.
Diagnosis: You're imagining things.
                That old problem: poor self-worth.

Then came the slammed door.
Birthday wishes unacknowledged.
(Not even an emoticon?
Is that company still...)
Follow-up email: In case you didn't get my....
Diagnosis: You were right.
                It's over.
And still that small green hope,
Pushing through the soil of other
Botched relationships:
It's that company...
No one checks email these days...

I'm about to try again
When I remember a time I
Slammed a door and stood
With my back against it,
Wishing it to stay closed,
Wishing the perseverer to disappear.

So I put away my phone.
I delete my email.
I turn to walk away

With an attempt at grace,
Aware even then that grace attempted
Is only clumsy pathos; and clumsy pathos
In retrospect is wounding bathos.

And I say to myself: 'Jerry, the world is big.
But in this corner, you have been forgotten.
No matter, there are other rooms, other hearts.
They will make up.'

I know they will.
This is not the first time.
Nor is it likely to be the last.
I have healed before.
Space has annealed before.

But still such puzzlement.
Because being puzzled is
A far more comfy space
Than the ordinary rut of hurt.

My Hotel Room at the Crowne Plaza, Dubai

(With thanks to the Dubai Literary Festival, who put me there.)

I love my hotel room.
It was not designed for me, I know.
It was designed for a tired businessman with sacks of dollars,
    a Saluki and two mistresses.
It is puzzled by me and I by it.
It wants to know why I am not watching the business news.
It wants to know why I have no laptop and no mobile phone
    and no phone calls
    that require me to stand by the window in a dressing
        gown,
    talking animated to Bill and Baab and Nihar and
        Ahmed.
Room 1654, this is for you.

Room, you are larger than my home.
Room, you have running water all 24 hours.
I wake up sometimes to dabble my fingers in fresh flowing streams.

Room, you offer me a view of a city, spread out like a gold souk.

Room, you have paintings, four of them, two in the toilet and
    I would study these paintings
    when I am on the pot but they are behind my head.

Room, you cost 1950 dirhams a day, not inclusive of
10 per cent municipal tax and 10 per cent
service tax and that's more than I have ever earned
from poetry.

Room, I can barely sleep here because I can't bear to think that
I might waste
even one dirham of that rental.

Room, your lights.
There's one near my bed, near my head which turns
itself on if I touch it.
I touch it.
I touch it, I touch it again.
I touch it on, off, on, off.
I'm a pervert.

Room, your air.
It's cool, it's clean, air as it should be.
I have a cold and a running nose.
My system is not used to this.

Room, your bed.
Should you be so yielding?
Have you no self-respect, room?
Come, let me go.

Room of four pillows, room of a minibar emptied before my
arrival in it because I have no credit card.

Room filled with chocolate bars and pistachio nuts that I
would be a fool to eat at those prices.

Room, I'm going to bed now. You should sleep too. Stop looking at me, room. And please, this transparent door, this picture window to the shower....Room, I'd like some privacy. Please.

Room? Room? Keep this between us, but I'm going to take the soap, the shampoo, the conditioner, the shower gel, the shower cap, the pencil, the pen, the envelopes, the writing pad, the tea bags, the coffee powder, the extra sugar, the soft slippers and
one big fat white beautiful virginal towel.

Learning from the Lockdown

From dust

The fan needs cleaning.
On top of each blade, a thick layer of dirt.
I think of the first particle of dust that settled there.
When the fan started it must have been whirled off.
But dust persists.

Dust gathers.
It sticks together.
Dust hangs on.

Can I learn from dust?

From swabbing

The first day I crouched to swab;
Because that's the best way, everyone says;
Because the best maids squat to swab, everyone knows.
My knees groaned all night.
The second day, I swabbed standing.

The third day, I decided swabbing
Every day was not really necessary.
Every alternate day will do it.

Can I be master to the maid
That I am to myself?

From ants

I set a plate down: soft cheese, hard tomato, boiled egg.
A black ant comes along, another, another.
'Good times, good times, food,' they signal each other.
'Mountains of food,' they tell each other.
All along the chain the message passes:
'Mountains of protein, mountains of food.'

I take my plate away.

The ants are perplexed.
Food? Mountain of food?
Where did it go?
Didn't you say...? Didn't we hear...?

A second later they're all searching again.

Can I learn from ants?

Acknowledgements

Some of these poems first appeared in *Poetry International*, *Literary Hub*, *Scroll.in* and *Poetly*. I thank the editors of all these magazines and journals.

ALSO FROM SPEAKING TIGER

ASYLUM
and other poems
Jerry Pinto

We lie quietly, listening.
The whales are singing each to each.
It is my last article of belief:
They understand their music.
You and I only have words.

Searching for safe havens; wanting to cut loose. Trying to make peace with death, love and madness. Learning that we can wound and be wounded. Looking for solace and meaning through rage and confusion.

Jerry Pinto's debut collection of poems, *Asylum* established him as a true original, a writer unafraid to be vulnerable, to take risks, to open the door and blunder into the world or let it sweep in. He travels, wrote Imtiaz Dharker, 'the breathtaking spaces between madness, luminosity and quiet rebellion... This is a writer who draws precise lines of control, and then, with surprising tenderness, crosses them.'